When in Doubt

TRUST GOD AND TAKE RESPONSIBILITY

Jason Nelson

Published by Straight Talk Books
P.O. Box 301, Milwaukee, WI 53201
800.661.3311 · timeofgrace.org

Printed in the United States of America
ISBN: 978-1-942107-43-9

About the Writer

Jason Nelson had a career as a teacher, counselor, and leader. He has a bachelor's degree in education, did graduate work in theology, and has a master's degree in counseling psychology. After his career ended in disabling back pain, he wrote the book *Miserable Joy: Chronic Pain in the Christian Life* (2007, Northwestern Publishing House). He has written and spoken extensively on a variety of topics related to the Christian life. Jason lives with his wife, Nancy, in Wisconsin.

About Time of Grace

Time of Grace is for people who want more growth and less struggle in their spiritual walk. Through the timeless truth of God's Word, we connect people to God's grace so they know they are loved and forgiven and so they can start living in the freedom they've always wanted.

To discover more, please visit timeofgrace.org or call 800.661.3311.

Help share God's message of grace!

Every gift you give helps Time of Grace reach people around the world with the good news of Jesus. Your generosity and prayer support take the gospel of grace to others through our ministry outreach and help them find the restart with Jesus they need.

Give today at timeofgrace.org/give or by calling 800.661.3311.

Thank you!

Contents

Preface

Near the end of my career I had a leadership position for a Christian school system. Unfamiliar clouds were gathering on the horizon. I felt it was my responsibility to help people recognize what was coming and be ready for change. After I gave a presentation to a large audience, a colleague challenged me. She said, "Jason, it seems like you are always trying to make us think outside the box." I responded with a smile, "I don't care if you think outside the box or inside the box; I just want you to think."

That is still my goal. I want us to think. And God wants us to think too. **"Finally, brothers and sisters, whatever is true, whatever is noble, whatever is right, whatever is pure, whatever is lovely, whatever is admirable—if anything is excellent or praiseworthy—think about such things"** (Philippians 4:8).

We all need to do more thinking. Thinking about what Jesus did for us. Thinking about what the Bible says to us. Thinking about our lives and our families and how to stay safe and prosper in a world that whirls right past the waypoints we use to navigate. Thinking leads to drawing conclusions. But we live in a world that defies coming to conclusions about so many things. Diversity among people produces strong differences of opinion. Advances in technology give people power over more things than they thought they had. History proves the unimaginable happens. This is the nature of change and generates doubt and uncertainty.

During times of doubt and uncertainty, I think we should be decisive. And I think we can trust God and take responsibility at the same time.

I plead with you to inform your thinking with the facts—always. I urge you to think for yourself. Please never outsource your thinking to anyone. And work hard to try to understand why other people think the way they do.

There was a time when the enduring ideas coming out of Europe and America were taken from or at least influenced by the Bible. People in the past lived in uncertain times too. But they kept thinking. And they articulated their thoughts in a way that shaped the world. God's narrative from beginning to end was the big story that provided the context, values, archetypes, and allusions for shared ideas that gave rise to civilization as we knew it.

Christian thought no longer dominates in the marketplace of ideas. It is just one of many alternatives. The comfort of a widely accepted way of looking at life is gone. Only a vague appreciation for godly ways is reflected in our culture. So we need to carry on the legacy of other Christians during other unsettling times. We need to do more thinking and express Christian ideas in fresh and convincing ways.

Aaron Nelson

The Perils of Uncertainty

I need to talk about the stress in my life. It's all from the tension between trusting God and taking personal responsibility. It's from the tug-of-war between depending on God and going it alone. It's from the dilemma of wanting to have childlike faith but needing to be a grown-up Christian.

When do we step up, and when do we stand down? There are reasons this is a tension in my life. And I suspect there are reasons it is a tension in yours. Just when I think I have found the balance, some profound change disrupts the equilibrium. Then what? When do we step up, and when do we stand down? When do we bow to God's providence, and when do we dig deeper and strive like we never have before?

Many years ago I consulted with a church that was having some problems. Offerings never kept up with expenses. Worship attendance was a small percentage of the membership. The buildings were in rough shape and needed to be repaired. Members were apathetic and divided over what should be done. Their story begins to illustrate my point. With unassailable spiritual priorities, the leaders embarked upon a campaign to get more people involved with Bible study.

Their rationale was sincere and faith filled. Since God's Word has power to change people and since those people needed changing, getting more of them into that Word would remedy everything. In fact, the preacher verbalized it. He said, "If we can just get more people in Bible class, *'everything else will take care of itself.'*" He expressed a notion held by many Christians. People should take responsibility for some things. But there are other things that we must just leave to God. Sticking our noses in there would be an affront to him and overstep a line we should not cross.

But are we always so sure where that line is? Are trust in God and taking responsibility exclusive of each other? Or in some cases do we best demonstrate our trust in God by taking even greater responsibility?

So the good people at this church embarked on a well-organized campaign to get more people involved in Bible study. Additional teachers were recruited, and classes were offered on Sunday morning, during the week, and in homes. Motivational addresses were given by leaders after services, urging everyone to take a Bible class. Large posters were placed conspicuously at the exits. You couldn't get out of the place without signing up for something. Attending Bible class became a holy epidemic.

And at the end of the year, offerings still didn't meet expenses. Worship attendance was a small percentage of the membership. The buildings were still shabby. And members were still not sure what they should do. One thing did change. A lot more people were in Bible classes. Their faith grew, and they were blessed because that's what they were clearly directed to do. Leaders took responsibility for that. But nothing else took care of itself.

God takes care of some things directly, and he takes care of some things through us. He makes the rain fall on the just and the unjust. And most days we get to decide what gets wet and what doesn't. We trust the Holy Spirit to create faith in that secret place where we believe. And he has given us the responsibility to proclaim the gospel energetically so that all people might be saved. It would seem that the more we trust that message the more we would be consumed by the sense of responsibility to bring it to others.

But some fine Christians choose to live passively in some areas of their lives and wear it as a badge of their trust in God. My parents were

God takes care of some things directly, and he takes care of some things through us.

like this when it came to managing money. They didn't have much, and they weren't forward thinking with what they had. They never owned a home. They didn't save or have any investments. My father thought he would work his whole life and then just die, which would take him off the hook for retirement planning. My mother sincerely believed that "God would provide." And when in old age they couldn't work and had very little to live on, God did provide. My wife and I took the responsibility to buy a house for them to live in. Their "trust" in God somehow allowed them to live in denial that a day of need was coming. Our trust in God moved us to go out on a limb to provide for them. We are not boasting. We never regretted doing it. But this helped me see the peril of being unprepared for the future and made me feel the tension between trusting God and taking responsibility. I learned something. The way some people trust forces other people to take even greater responsibility.

God should be trusted. His works compel it. His Word calls for it. It is relevant to every issue in our lives. The Holy Spirit works through that Word in amazing ways. One story tells of an evangelist who felt a calling to minister to the homeless. He spent months in the streets preaching fire, brimstone, and Jesus to lost souls. After one spellbinder of a sermon, a young street person came up to the preacher and asked if he could have his Bible. The preacher got a shiver and wanted to take the young man to the next spiritual mile marker. But the man said, "Nah, I just noticed that the pages of your Bible were real thin and I could use them to roll a smoke." So the quick-thinking preacher cut him a deal. He said, "I will give you my Bible if you promise to read each page before you smoke it."

Sometime later a young man came up to the preacher. The preacher recognized him as the one to whom he had given his Bible. But this time the young man was clean-shaven, well-groomed, and clear-eyed. The preacher asked him what had changed. The young man said, "Well, I kept our deal. I smoked Matthew. I smoked Mark. I smoked Luke. And then John smoked me."

The Word of God has smoked a lot of people. Time spent studying by ourselves and discussing the Bible with others is the foundation for building a Christian life. The Bible reorders our thinking with wisdom that is in stark contrast to anything else available. It never contradicts itself but is filled with taut alternatives that are like harp strings upon which the Holy Spirit plays themes that energize us. These become intensely personal anthems of Scripture searching and soul searching, especially when we are confronted with uncertainty.

With God, things just don't lay out the way we would expect them to. In fact, he alerted us to this tendency. He warned us straight up: **"'My thoughts are not your thoughts, neither are your ways my ways,' declares the** Lord. **'As the heavens are higher than the earth, so are my ways higher than your ways and my thoughts than your thoughts'"** (Isaiah 55:8,9).

In our way of thinking, it would seem that if we want to be noticed, we should be noticeable. If we want to end up in first place, we should be self-promoting. Just watch schoolkids line up for lunch. No one is shoving his or her way to the end of the line. But according to God's way of thinking, the last shall be first. The spiritual race is to the back of the line. And because there is generally so much room there, it is easy to be noticed. Humble, heartfelt service is the key to success. **"Have the same mindset as Christ Jesus: who, being in very nature God, did not consider equality with God something to be used to his own advantage; rather, he made himself nothing by taking the very nature of a servant. He humbled himself by becoming obedient to death—even death on a cross! Therefore God exalted him to the highest place"** (Philippians 2:5–9).

When we take the responsibility to honor God with our best effort, it will be noticed by God. Our dependability and character will be noticed by others. The less concerned we are about ourselves, the more others recognize something special in us.

I know that worry is quicksand. But mindless surrender is not the same as trust. We don't save spiritual energy by turning off the lights. That could lead us to stop reevaluating things that can be reevaluated. It takes an engaged

Mindless surrender is not the same as trust.

mind to meditate on God's Word day and night and make decisions in response to challenges. If we don't, we rob ourselves of up-to-the-minute insight. We become reactive instead of proactive. Opportunities get lost. Problems gain momentum. Letting go and letting God could be a risky alternative to trusting God and taking responsibility.

Jesus is **"the way and the truth and the life"** (John 14:6). There is no doubt about that. But living as his people is complicated. And what makes our lives most complicated is other people. It is the presence of other people in our lives that puts our trust in God and sense of responsibility to the greatest test.

"This is how God showed his love among us: He sent his one and only Son into the world that we might live through him" (1 John 4:9). And he is counting on us to express that love to others on his behalf. **"No one has ever seen God; but if we love one another, God lives in us and his love is made complete in us"** (1 John 4:12). One of the most God-loving things we can do is love others deeply, from the heart.

So we get ahead *by* serving others. We show our love for God *by* loving others. And we demonstrate our trust in God *by* being incredibly responsible because in this life, nothing takes care of itself.

A Page for You

What is God taking care of through you?

What uncertainties create tension for you?

How can you avoid the perils of uncertainty by placing greater trust in God?

How can you avoid the perils of uncertainty by taking greater responsibility?

Any other thoughts?

When in Doubt
Trust God and Take Responsibility for Yourself

The human life cycle is a drama in learning to trust God and learning to take responsibility. The journey is invigorating because the scenes are always changing. God doesn't change. But we do, and so do the circumstances of our lives. Along the way he gives us both direction and permission in a life he is intimately involved with and lets us manage for ourselves.

"All the world's a stage, and all the men and women merely players; they have their exits and their entrances, and one man in his time plays many parts, his acts being seven ages" (William Shakespeare, *As You Like It*, Act 2, Scene 7).

Shakespeare and others have described the developmental nature of being human. The progression from one stage of life to another is the stuff of poetry and psychology. Making it all the way through is a good life. Breaking down along the way demands that we adjust how we trust God and be responsible. Each stage suggests its own theme and creates very distinct challenges.

Exploring

"At first, the infant, mewling and puking in the nurse's arms" (Shakespeare, *As You Like It*).

"When I was a child, I spoke like a child, I thought like a child, I reasoned like a child. When I became a man, I gave up childish ways" (1 Corinthians 13:11 ESV).

God wants every baby to land in the arms of a loving mother. Life can't get off to a better start than that. It is a baby's job to be difficult and recklessly explore the nature of the universe. Someone else has to be responsible. That is an enormous test for caregivers. You have to watch 'em like a hawk. You probably shouldn't have one until you're up to the task. Don't be fooled by cute and sweet. These little bundles can explode on you.

> God wants every baby to land in the arms of a loving mother.

Very early on, every parent has to find the balance between taking good care of their children and teaching their children to take care of themselves. Detaching too soon is neglect. Hanging on too long is misplaced dependency. Good parents have a knack for getting this right.

It is a child's responsibility to play. It is a child's responsibility to imagine wonderful things and say precious things because they see beautiful things. It is a child's responsibility to lose track of time because they are in the flow of their own creativity. They trust someone else will put food on the table, buy toothpaste and soap, and remind them to use it. And if some of their curiosity can linger into later life, they can be innovators, inventors, and entrepreneurs. Children are responsible for dreams.

Jesus loves children. He held them and blessed them. He said, **"Let the little children come to me, and do not hinder them, for the kingdom of heaven belongs to such as these"** (Matthew 19:14). He had no tolerance for any kind of abuse of children. **"If anyone causes one of these little ones—those who believe in me—to stumble, it would be better for them to have a large millstone hung around their neck and to be drowned in the depths of the sea"** (Matthew 18:6). He said they were the greatest in the kingdom of heaven, and he aligned himself with them. **"And whoever welcomes one such child in my name welcomes me"** (Matthew 18:5).

We all have to give up childish ways eventually. It is a tragedy that so many children in the world are forced to put away childhood prematurely because they don't have the safety and necessities to enjoy it. If you are a child today anywhere in the world, you are more likely than not to be poor and unhappy for all kinds of reasons. And there is nothing you can do about it.

Jesus made himself perfectly clear: **"See that you do not despise one of these little ones. For**

I tell you that their angels in heaven always see the face of my Father in heaven" (Matthew 18:10). So who is responsible for the children? We are, because they can't be responsible for themselves. They can only trust that someone will do something. How would the world be better if we made decisions based on what is best for children, if we kept their trust in us for Jesus' sake?

When I was a young parent, an artist in my church gave my wife and me a beautiful present. She did an exquisite chalk portrait of the face of my baby daughter cheek-to-cheek with the face of Jesus. As lovely as the piece was, the real gift was that it changed forever how I view children. I will always see the face of Jesus cuddled against the face of every child. I am pleading with you to do the same. His words need to ring in our ears. **"Whatever you did for one of the least of these brothers and sisters of mine, you did for me"** (Matthew 25:40). Let us shoulder together the responsibility for making this world a better place for children. It will be a better place for everyone.

Learning

"Then the whining schoolboy, with his satchel and shining morning face, creeping like snail unwillingly to school" (Shakespeare, *As You Like It*).

"Remember not the sins of my youth or my transgressions; according to your steadfast love

remember me, for the sake of your goodness, O LORD!"
(Psalm 25:7 ESV).

There are still cultures where life is portioned into two stages, childhood and adulthood. Historically that was the pattern. Passage from one stage to the other occurred when a young person got through puberty and became capable of sexually reproducing. The ability to have sex and make a baby made a person an adult. When this occurred, girls were given in marriage and boys took a wife. Kind of like Mary and Joseph. Then they both took up the duties of being adults, whatever that meant. It usually meant spending nearly every waking hour making sure your family survived. Before that, childhood was spent learning what it took to survive.

Adolescence is an outgrowth of modern industrialization. The prohibition of child labor in sweatshops and the development of high school education created a stage of life between childhood and adulthood. Human brain development accommodated the change and put itself on hold for a while. We now give children the leisure of four or more years to figure out how to become adults. We have learned to excuse them for being irresponsible, and we rationalize a lot of inappropriate behavior as age typical. We have created a high school experience that is as social—and activity oriented—as it is academic. Then we tell them you're only young once so have fun. Many of them are having fun, or so it seems.

I spent 12 years of my life working with teenagers as a high school counselor and high school principal. I loved them. Their energy and optimism were contagious. So were their struggles. Anyone who has ever loved a teenager knows whatever they go through, you go through. If they trust you, they will tell you anything. They will tell you they aren't having that much fun and really don't know what to do about it. They are confused, and they confuse us. They can make you proud when they take responsibility. They can break your heart when hormones and emotions overrun their tentative self-discipline.

They learn at school when it is relevant and outside of school because it's always relevant. A hero and villain live in the same skin. They build identity by imitating what they see because they see better than they think. They respect authority that returns the favor. Some freely express themselves on any topic with the same vulgar word. Never underestimate how savvy they really are. They remember what they experience

Anyone who has ever loved a teenager knows whatever they go through, you go through.

because it is so intense. And they will be responsible for the world that I grow old in.

Most teenagers act like they will be one all of their lives. And most adults act like they never were one. There's the rub. Neither recognizes the quick passage into and out of this time of life. Battles rage over very temporary issues. Everyone's perspective will change. Hopefully, no permanent damage is done to relationships along the way.

I love seeing the class reunion pictures in my small-town paper. I am always curious about the back story. How did they deal with the awkward moments of facing each other after all those years? It appears that the survivors of adolescence have turned out fine and made peace with their pasts and each other, probably by forgetting, which is easier after 40 years. Adolescence is about learning unforgettable lessons, learning what you need to forget, and praying, "Dear Lord, I trust that you have forgotten too."

Loving

"And then the lover, sighing like furnace, with a woeful ballad made to his mistress' eyebrow" (Shakespeare, *As You Like It*).

"How can a young man keep his way pure? By guarding it according to your word. With my whole heart I seek you; let me not wander from your commandments!" (Psalm 119:9,10 ESV).

Adult life is a crowded canvas upon which we squeeze in new images and establish new patterns. It is cluttered with everything we have been. But each transition, no matter how difficult or disappointing, opens up some fresh space. Change stretches the fabric of our lives. It creates opportunities to become more of what God would have us be.

Adulthood seems to be coming on more slowly than ever. Sociologists are identifying yet another intervening stage of life. The *New York Times* raised the question, *What Is It About 20-Somethings?* (August 18, 2010). By and large these are talented and attractive young people. They are culturally diverse, open, personable, and perpetually making progress. Often they are well educated with degrees that make them confident but not easily employable. And the jobs they do find may not pay that well. They carry a lot of school debt. They may be living at home longer or more often than they should but prefer to hang with friends in little tribes. **Change stretches the fabric of our lives.** They want to marry someday but are delaying it until they are sure they can make it work. In the meantime, they are sexually active. They like extreme sports, going to bars, playing drinking games, and dabbling with drugs. They seem to prefer the contrivances of reality TV to the hard realities of life itself.

They are the subjects of society's experiment to peg the onset of adulthood. The starting point is unclear. In most of America, a person can drive at age 16, vote at 18, buy alcohol at 21, rent a car at 25, and stay on their parents' health insurance until 26.

When is a person really an adult?

An overwhelming sense of possibilities and overblown passions keep many emerging adults churning in place. They still don't know what they want to be now that they are grown up. This corresponds to what we now know about brain development. Emotions from an exploding limbic system come on strong during puberty. But the brain doesn't completely wire the prefrontal cortex until a person is in their mid to late 20s. That is where rational decision-making and managing emotions occur. That is the part of the brain that enables us to follow through on our good intentions.

But brilliant things happen when young, red-hot lovers pull it together and pursue their passions with their whole hearts. It becomes their responsibility. Mark Zuckerberg started Facebook. Taylor Swift became a superstar. And back in the day Mother Teresa took her vows.

What are the marks of a maturing Christian? **"For this very reason, make every effort to add to your faith goodness; and to goodness, knowledge; and to knowledge, self-control; and to self-control, perseverance; and to perseverance, godliness; and to godliness, mutual affection; and to mutual affection, love. For if you possess these qualities in increasing measure, they will keep you from being ineffective and unproductive in your knowledge of our Lord Jesus Christ"** (2 Peter 1:5-8).

Emerging adulthood is a heavy lift away from childish and adolescent behavior. Jesus carried that old, rugged cross so that we can participate in godliness through faith in him. His love compels conscious, determined effort from us to grow in faithful living every step of the way. We start asking ourselves the right questions. "What kind of woman do I want to be?" "What kind of man do I want to be?" God answers. Take stock of who you are and add to what you are. It is a highly reflective process. We seek his will with our whole heart; cleanse our waywardness in Jesus' blood; and add big measures of knowledge, self-control, perseverance, kindness, and love to our character. Then we can be increasingly effective and productive.

Working

"Then a soldier, full of strange oaths and bearded like the pard, jealous in honor, sudden and quick in quarrel, seeking the bubble reputation even in the cannon's mouth" (Shakespeare, *As You Like It*).

"But as for you, O man of God, flee these things. Pursue righteousness, godliness, faith, love, steadfastness, gentleness. Fight the good fight of the faith. Take hold of the eternal life to which you were called and about which you made the good confession in the presence of many witnesses" (1 Timothy 6:11,12 ESV).

Some days it is all such a battle. There are so many fronts, so many things to take care of. Staying fit, being a family, serving at church, volunteering in the community, and doing a good job at work put lots of stress on men and women who fight this battle every single day. How can we honor all of the commitments? How do we keep all of the promises?

Much of it revolves around going to work. Responsible Christian adults deploy their faith and build their reputations in the workplace as much as anywhere. That is where we prove we are salt and light in front of supervisors, coworkers, and customers. That is where we get rewarded for our effort. That is where we use our talents, develop new ones, and advance through the ranks because we are dependable. It is our useful calling.

Working people can struggle to hold it all together.

Working people can struggle to hold it all together. The stakes are high. People are counting on us to get the job done and provide for them. There is a lot of weight on our shoulders, and there are bumps in the road. Periods of satisfaction get interrupted by chaos. We second-guess ourselves, our ability, and our career choice. Maybe we are just not cut out for this gig. The helplessness we feel at times confirms a supernatural reality. We are creatures: advanced creatures—but still creatures. We bang our heads against the confining walls of our *creatureliness* every single day. C. S. Lewis observed that we just won't surrender self-will as long as all is well (*The Problem of Pain*). All isn't always well. Stuff happens, and we are responsible. And we feel inadequate and uncertain.

Ironically, feeling small is essential to personal and professional growth. We can give up or we can grow. We can take responsibility for our own development. When our careers stall, we trust God's promise. **"'I know the plans I have for you,' declares the** Lord**, 'plans to prosper you and not to harm you, plans to give you hope and a future'"** (Jeremiah 29:11). He has work for us to do. He has plans for us. The problem is he's not real direct in letting us know what they are. He doesn't pierce our noses, clip leashes to them, and drag us where he wants us to go. He grants us the liberty and ability to make plans for ourselves and then to try to align them with his plans for us. This is tricky. He is very interested and active in what we do. He influences us in a mighty way with the teachings of the Bible. He sends others into our lives to try to interrupt a wrong choice or to encourage us along a right path. He often clears the way toward what pleases him and puts barricades in the middle of the road to a train wreck. And sometimes he simply

He grants us the liberty and ability to make plans for ourselves and then to try to align them with his plans for us.

gives us a feeling that just won't let go.

After years of trial and error, I have come to believe this. The closer I can get my plans for myself to God's plans for me, the better things go. And when my plans for myself don't line up with God's plans for me, the more trouble I have.

The working warriors in our society talk about what they do on the job more than anything else. Their job titles are their identity. The great tragedy in getting a pink slip is that it sucks the meaning out of life. Getting up every day to go to the job can be a grind. I hear people say they can't wait until they don't have to do it anymore. But I say, be careful what you wish for. Solomon said, **"There is nothing better for people to do than to eat, drink, and find satisfaction in their work. I saw that even this comes from the hand of God"** (Ecclesiastes 2:24 GW).

Serving

"And then the justice, in fair round belly with good capon lined, with eyes severe and beard of formal cut, full of wise saws and modern instances; and so he plays his part" (Shakespeare, *As You Like It*).

"Deacons likewise must be dignified, not double-tongued, not addicted to much wine, not greedy for dishonest gain. They must hold the mystery of the faith with a clear conscience. And let them also be tested first;

then let them serve as deacons if they prove themselves blameless" (1 Timothy 3:8–10 ESV).

Eventually we get to a stage of life when it becomes obvious we've had too many chicken dinners. Hopefully it is just as obvious that we have been around the block. We've learned a thing or two. This isn't our first rodeo. We weren't born yesterday. You know what I'm talking about?

There is a blessing granted to us as we mature. People trust us. That is an honor and a sobering responsibility. It takes some serious emotional and spiritual growth to set aside self-interest and pursue the greater good. It takes some authentic ego strength to put others first. It takes a great deal of security in one's self to encourage the success of others and mentor them along the way.

Mature Christians speak with authority because they have experience. They can express consistent points of view because they have put ideas to the test over time and generally know their own minds. They know what works and

Mature Christians speak with authority because they have experience.

what doesn't. They contribute good judgment to families, businesses, organizations, and churches. They can connect the dots and provide continuity in performance. They know history and don't want to relive it. And they can interpret life according to God's will. They are able to see him at work in good times and in bad. They attribute good outcomes to the hand of the Lord with the confidence born of a lifetime of faith.

But there's a downside to having seen it all before. Aging people can become cynical. Recollection of disappointments can lead to expecting the worst. The accumulated effect of dealing with human flaws fuels suspicion and negativity toward others. Battle fatigue can make older folks wary of new initiatives. Physical discomfort can make them cranky. They can frustrate the enthusiasm of younger colleagues whom they see as the naive faces of recycled ideas that won't pan out. Their bluntness can hurt feelings and stifle progress. They can resist change because they tried it before and it didn't work.

Perhaps the ultimate responsibility of mature adults is assessing how much gas is still in their own tanks. Because of experience, veteran workers, managers, and leaders can be very efficient. They are quick studies and can be productive without spinning their wheels or wasting time learning by trial and error. Their brains are structured with well-developed neural pathways. They can approach a task in a direct line and can deftly eliminate wasted motions. They know what shortcuts they can take and still get the job done well.

But after a while, a path of shortcuts becomes a slippery slope. Productivity is confined to the energy level of an aging person. The work gets reduced to what a tired person can handle. This is an insidious process. No malice intended. It happens a little at a time. But eventually it is noticeable that we just aren't what we used to be and can't do what we used to do. Hanging in there is no longer good service but may be unintended selfishness enabled by seniority. When is it time? This is a tough call we need to make ourselves or someone will be left with the responsibility to make it for us. No one wants to tell the person everyone admires to move on. No one wants to pull the plug on people who should go out on their own terms and be honored for their service. It hurts to watch heroes fade. After decades of effectively solving problems for others, it would be tragic to become one.

Resting

"The sixth age shifts into the lean and slipper'd pantaloon, with spectacles on nose and pouch on side, his youthful hose, well sav'd, a world too wide for his shrunk shank; and his big manly voice, turning again toward childish treble, pipes and whistles in his sound" (Shakespeare, *As You Like It*).

"Wisdom is with the aged, and understanding in length of days" (Job 12:12 ESV).

Have you seen these guys? They show up at the convenience store first thing in the morning in their comfy pants for a coffee, donut, and newspaper. And when these relaxed dudes go shopping with their wives, they sit in the geezer chair just outside the ladies' dressing room where they can doze a little and steer clear of the unspeakable things going on behind all those curtains. Their eyes twinkle with delight over little things, and their voices are charming whispers of what they used to be. Younger women still find them cute—like teddy bears.

Sometimes it is just good to rest. I have seen people struggle with the idea of retiring. That decision is more complicated than it used to be. It seems that people are living longer, so it follows they may want to work longer. Pension plans are structured to give an incentive to wait and draw larger checks later in life. Some people are still vigorous and enjoy their careers. Some people have no idea what they would do if they weren't working. The last thing anyone wants is to be put out to pasture.

Sometimes it is just good to rest.

I became physically disabled during what should have been my prime. I never really had to make the decision to retire. But I have dealt with some of the same issues. I still struggle with figuring out how to pass the time. Some days getting an oil change is the high point. And I get lonely and miss the camaraderie of the workplace. I have also discovered that the opportunity to rest when I need to allows me to continue to be productive.

The purpose of rest is renewal. It accommodates physical, spiritual, and emotional healing. That's why things look better in the morning. Having time allows for reflection and sharing wisdom. Here is a tidbit for the young bucks and does. As you are pursuing your vocation, work at cultivating an avocation. Develop a hobby, a favorite pastime, an alter ego. It will refresh you now and will come in handy later. I'm glad I like to fish.

I have a tendency to want to rescue useful things discarded by others. I enjoy the challenge of figuring out what I can do with them. I once made some very functional note holders out of old mousetraps screwed to a board. I have stopped my vehicle to pick up a bungee cord or two and orphaned boat cushions. I know my kids are afraid I will become that guy who buries an old bathtub in his front yard to use as a planter. So I am trying to use restraint.

But I think there is a reason that people of a certain age do things like that. It is an object lesson for their lives. By the time we get a handle on the purpose of our lives, it is time to repurpose our lives. It is time to use our remaining time and energy to do something else fulfilling.

I have always liked George Herbert Walker Bush. His long and heroic career in public service is admirable. He has been the husband of one wife and raised a good family. His one term as president gets mixed reviews. But what sets him apart from others is his approach to life after his presidency.

As an octogenarian, he parachuted out of airplanes. This was much more than a publicity stunt. It was emblematic of a striving philosophy of life. It is an example for all of us who are tempted to believe our best days are behind us.

Each of us is in one stage of life and heading for another. The day may come when we can no longer take responsibility for ourselves. So until someone takes the parachute away from you—jump.

Passing

"Last scene of all, that ends this strange eventful history, is second childishness and mere oblivion; sans teeth, sans eyes, sans taste, sans everything" (Shakespeare, *As You Like It*).

"I have been young, and now am old, yet I have not seen the righteous forsaken or his children begging for bread" (Psalm 37:25 ESV).

My father is one of my heroes. He accomplished the most difficult feat in the human experience. He changed for the better. Certainly he did it with the help of God and the love of a good woman. Nevertheless, a life of struggles ended with him being transformed because he trusted God and took responsibility for himself.

He survived many critical health problems longer than anyone expected and lived in discomfort most of his later life. When he was given the news that cancer had now taken over his other lung and that he had a short time to live, he remained absolutely true to form. He expressed the same mild level of personal disappointment that he did when he would find out his car was on the fritz. *"Oh, no."*

Then with his trademark way of striking up a conversation, he would tell people about it. He would cheerfully approach the people he knew. *"Did you hear? I'm passing away. You better come to my funeral."* Or when I took him to the grocery store, he would engage in his usual banter with the checker, look at me, and ask, *"Jason, did you tell her I am passing away?"* For him, it was just one more way to try to joke around, to connect with others and be the center of attention.

The last scene of his life was very intense. At first, I don't think he felt like he was dying. He was still feisty and with his usual cynicism he would say, *"I hope that doctor knows what he is talking about."* He was always impatient that this was taking longer than he expected. But when the end came, it came quickly. I would talk about heaven with him as often as I could. He would say, *"I hope I make it."* Right to the end he struggled with trusting God's grace. He seemed suspicious that God would still hold the sins of his past life against him. He felt betrayed by authority his whole life. This was as big as it gets. But we would remind him over and over again, *"This is why Jesus died."*

In the final days he fought death. Not because he was afraid but because he didn't want my mom to be left alone. He had become caretaker for both of them.

One day was especially difficult. He was incoherent, defiant, extremely weak, and very restless. It was more than we could handle. He needed to be in a hospice but refused to go. He also needed to urinate but couldn't make it to the bathroom. I sat on the bed next to him, raised him up in my arms, and helped him urinate in a bottle. I never thought taking responsibility could come to this.

God granted peace the next morning. My dad was calm and agreed to go to the hospice house. He made the paramedics stop the gurney. He gave my mom a final kiss and said, *"I just didn't want to spend my last days away from my wife."* The family gathered around him that night in the very nice but unfamiliar room where he would die. We told him that we loved him. We told him that Jesus loved him. He said, *"I know"* and that he loved us. He was so thin and frail. His dentures were on the bed table and his face was hollow. We tried to interact with him, but it was very difficult. He was in and out of consciousness. As we were leaving and saying good-bye, my daughter held his great-granddaughter in front of his face. He opened his eyes, raised his head, flashed a big toothless smile, and whispered, *"Abigail."* His final smile was for his new great-granddaughter. And he passed in peace.

If we have been devoted to God with a conscience unstrapped from guilt through Jesus

> **I never thought taking responsibility could come to this.**

Christ, we don't pass into oblivion. We don't just stop existing. We don't evaporate into the great unknown. We pass in peace, and God welcomes us home with affirmation. **"Well done, good and faithful servant! . . . Come and share your master's happiness!"** (Matthew 25:21).

A Page for You

What stage of life are you in?

What doubts do you have about yourself?

What tough decisions do you need to make?

What words of Jesus hit home for you?

What have you learned about life that you can share with others?

What legacy would you like to leave behind?

When in Doubt
Trust God and Take Responsibility for a Strong Family

There is no remedy for life's problems. There is no miracle cure for what ails the world either. But if there was, it would be that everyone lives in a healthy home. So when in doubt about everything else, trust God and take responsibility for a strong family.

The family is the bridge between the individual and the rest of the world. Everything that happens in the family has a profound influence on how people make their way in life. Destroying a family should be a crime. Disrupting a family should at least be a misdemeanor because every aspect of society suffers the consequences. Healthy people and hurting people leave some kind of family every day to function in other venues. Escaping from a house of horrors to go somewhere else may seem like a relief, but it is a temporary one. The psychological goblins follow us out the door and cling to us like monkeys on our backs. Leaving a safe, secure home is the greatest start to any day, and returning there is the happiest ending.

When God announced it was not good for man to be alone, it wasn't because Adam needed a playmate. He needed a soul mate. So the family was born. And marriage was created as its core. Adam was no longer alone. Eve was bone of his bone, flesh of his flesh, with a mind to understand his and a heart for him only. They had bodies that were designed to fit together nicely and could make love face-to-face. That's a marriage.

It is relatively easy to get married and, as it turns out, unmarried. But it takes work to make a marriage. Having a wedding and making a marriage are two entirely different things. The word *marriage* connotes coming together in a made-for-each-other kind of way. How tragic when a woman and man have a wedding but never make a marriage. This will sound a little goofy, but I think the divorce rate could be reduced if people would just stay married longer, if they would trust God and take responsibility for each other one more day.

The marriage relationship is the sunshine or the dark cloud hovering over each family. The mood of the marriage is the climate for the home. Family isn't about the kids. It isn't about the in-laws. It isn't about appearances at church or stature in the community. Family is about the marriage.

The mood of the marriage is the climate for the home.

Nothing deserves more attention than the marriage relationship, yet it is appalling how little thought we give to it.

There are advantages and disadvantages to marrying young. The trend is headed the other direction for many sociological reasons. I understand those reasons. Today's young adults have seen so many failed marriages that they are waiting to get it right. Getting on the career path takes longer than it used to. They like hanging out with their friends and don't want to ruin a good friendship by marrying one. They know marriage will cramp their style. But as the marrying age goes up, so do the complications. With each and every passing year of single adulthood, people have more invested in themselves. So they have more to consider before divesting some of it and reinvesting in someone else. I am not suggesting young adults should rush into marriage. But I am suggesting that there are real advantages to committing to another and maturing together in marriage.

Some adults are very fulfilled as single people. Some single adults would like to be married. I know from listening to them that as they get older, they hear the clock ticking. It is the sound of time running out. A lot of other fears complicate establishing and maintaining promising relationships. The older we get, the more experience we have. The more experience we have, the more we have to think about. The more we have to think about, the less able we are to give in to love.

Whether we are in a marriage or hoping for one, we can trust God as we take responsibility to make it work. God is the expert at wiping the slate clean and making everything new. Jesus' death and resurrection give us eternal life and regular fresh starts in this one. His Word and Spirit can rewrite history.

We are all in some kind of private bondage. We are all coming out of some kind of haunting captivity. What he promised his children lost in Babylon is a word for all of us who live in our own personal exile.

"I will take you out of the nations; I will gather you from all the countries and bring you back into your own land. I will sprinkle clean water on you, and you will be clean; I will cleanse you from all your impurities and from all your idols. I will give you a new heart and put a new spirit in you; I will remove from you your heart of stone and give you a heart of flesh" (Ezekiel 36:24–26).

Hearts of stone repel everything. They have been calcified by every sin we have committed and others have committed against us. They reject the love of God. They resist the love of another. But a heart of flesh brings the best of being human to every relationship. Hearts of flesh are tender. They have faith. They are teachable. They are pliable. They are real. They hurt. They are vulnerable. They give. They forgive. And they beat on. Marriages are made and sustained with hearts of flesh.

From the beginning, God gave some very practical guidance for marriage: **"That is why a man leaves his father and mother and is united to his wife, and they become one flesh"** (Genesis

2:24). But early on there is almost nothing said about raising children. Surely God knew that children change everything. Had things gone as God intended, I can imagine Adam scolding, "Hey, you kids, get away from that tree." Apparently God figured if the marriage was right, child-rearing wouldn't be much of a problem. At least not in paradise.

After the fall nothing was as right as it used to be. And the effect on Cain and Abel was disastrous. But the power of a good marriage traveled outside of paradise. It is not to be underestimated. Father Theodore Hesburgh famously said, "The most important thing a father can do for his children is love their mother." The first rule of parenting is to love your spouse. And when you just don't know what to do with your kids, love your spouse even more because love never fails.

Parents love their children. And they need to lead them. For me, those are the essential dimensions in raising children. Loving and leading are the intersecting lines along which we take parental responsibility. Loving is everything we bring into our parenting and our relationships with our children. It

The first rule of parenting is to love your spouse.

includes affection for them, affirmation of them, and patience with them. It includes that swell of pride we get every time we look at them and the nurturing we do every day. Love is expressed in mundane things like doing the laundry and profound things like forgiving and restoring them to their special place in the family when they break the rules and our hearts. *We love them when we bring the best of who we are into our parenting.*

Leading captures everything we bring out of our parenting. It starts with our example. We lead our children when we consistently live out the values we have taught them. We lead them when we are careful to discipline them. We lead them when we direct them toward God's purposes for their lives. Our leadership as parents provides a sense of direction for the entire family. It is clear, courageous, and contagious. *We lead them when we bring the best of who they are out of our parenting.*

Dutiful Parents

Different parents take different approaches to parenting. There are parents who lead much more than they express love. They parent out of duty. It is their responsibility whether their hearts are in it or not. They tend to be authoritarian. They lay down the rules. And they expect strict compliance. The punishment for failure can be severe, even physical. They bring a lot out of their parenting. These controlling parents produce compliant and compulsive children who have learned they get approval by earning it, and they work very hard to earn it. These children can be very low maintenance and very high achievers. Being strict parents isn't bad. But, it can go too far. The worst case of this kind of parenting is physical abuse of children masquerading as discipline.

Dependent Parents

Some parents love much more than they lead. They are overly sensitive to what happens to their children. They depend on their children to fill some big holes in their own lives and are afraid that if they lead too much, their children won't like them anymore. These parents need their children more than their children need them. Their management of their children is manipulative. They promise rewards that smell like bribes. They heap loads of guilt on their kids because of how their children's behavior reflects on them. They defend their kids to a fault and enable their kids to get away with more than they should. They produce confused and incompetent children who are unsure whether it is about them or Mom and Dad. They wonder, *"Are my parents supposed to meet my needs or am I supposed to meet theirs?"* The obscenest form of this kind of parenting is incest, where parents need children to satisfy their sexual needs.

Detached Parents

Some parents aren't able to lead much and aren't able to express love much because they are preoccupied with themselves. The sad fact is they are detached from their children. They can be permissive as a way of keeping the children from interfering with their own lives. "Do what you want. Just don't bother me." They neglect to do the hard work of establishing boundaries, enforcing the rules, or maybe even providing for their children's basic needs. When the child tries to get noticed or discover the boundaries, the parents don't respond. They are too busy or self-involved. Over time, their children become distant, defiant, and deeply angry. Trying to be noticed and not getting noticed day after day makes kids really angry. In the worst case some parents abandon their children. They just take off and leave their kids behind. It doesn't get more detached than that.

Discipling Parents

And some parents make disciples of their children. Their love for their children is healthy and unconditional, and their leadership of their children is courageous and clear. They exercise their God-given authority without going on a power trip. They are self-sacrificing as Christ was. They are mature people and secure in their Lord, their relationship with others, and themselves. It is their own maturity that enables them to lead their children into maturity. Their skill in parenting allows them to produce confident and compassionate children.

Their goal is not to have nice obedient children, codependent children, or children who don't get in the way. Their goal is to have children who become high functioning Christian adults, and they empower their children toward that goal with the love and leadership they demonstrate. Children in these homes blossom because day after day they can depend on their parents to be more mature than they are.

"God sets the lonely in families" (Psalm 68:6) and things that feel like families. Good neighborhoods, workplaces, athletic teams, congregations, and other groups of people can feel like home. It is a blessing to be part of one. Some people find in them what they never found at home. Some people's lives have been rescued by being part of something that feels like a family.

And there are variations on the family itself. I have deep admiration for the single parent who does a two-person job alone. I respect the stepparents who love other people's children as their own. Some children who were born into something far less are adopted into families that love them deeply. God continues to place the lonely in some kind of family where there is loving and leading. And if people can grow in any of these later family types, it is because they have borrowed something very fertile from the original.

A Page for You

Draw a picture of your family. You can use stick people. Name each person and arrange them to illustrate their distance from home and each other. Draw solid lines, bold lines, dashed lines, or no lines to connect people and illustrate the strength of family members' relationships with each other.

What do you see? Is Jesus in the picture? What would you like to see? What responsibility can you take to make your family stronger?

When in Doubt
Trust God and Take Responsibility Where No One Else Will

I invite you to wander into a metaphor with me. Life is filled with gardens and every garden needs tending. Some people are content to garden in the interior of life. It is safe and comfortable there. The ground is easier to work because it has been worked over many times before. The traces of other's footprints or fingerprints don't bother these people. Interior people have the gift of contentment and a knack for capitalizing on their predecessor's work.

There is biblical appreciation for this kind of gardening: **"I planted the seed, Apollos watered it, but God has been making it grow"** (1 Corinthians 3:6). Like Apollos, some people are good middlemen and women. They keep things going. Interior gardeners live happily within the boundaries of the garden they were given. Their satisfaction is in a predictable and manageable harvest. They are good followers.

But there are others who just can't garden there. They are restless in the interior. They are unfulfilled with the status quo. They are drawn to the edges. They understand that God also uses people to make things grow. They have a yearning to be one of them. They feel responsible for things others may not. They are good leaders.

Before Jesus gave his disciples the responsibilities of leadership, he called, "Follow me." They spent three years in his footsteps, listened to his teaching, and saw the signs and wonders. Yet they struggled with the good act of following. They struggled to understand the Messiah. They struggled to fully grasp the purpose of his life, the necessity of his crucifixion, the triumph of his resurrection, and the commission he gave them at his ascension. These men and women followed Jesus to the edge. An edge they never fully understood but that they believed gave their lives eternal significance because of the Spirit they caught from Jesus.

Robert Browning said that some people's reach exceeds their grasp. These folks can wear us out. It is easy to become irritated with their endless prodding. It is tempting to ignore them as being unrealistic. But God makes good use of far-reaching people. Without far-reaching people, America would never have become the new world. We would live in fear of our children contracting polio. We would need horse barns instead of garages. And we would not be taking so many forms of technology for granted. Far-reaching people serve the rest of us in a way we don't

God makes good use of far-reaching people.

always appreciate. They make the garden bigger. They enlarge the interior. They have politely or not so politely resisted the inertia that keeps many there. Their contrarian tendency causes them to look at things another way. They raise questions and lift the sight line. They interpret the edge to be the horizon.

Living on the edge has gotten a bad name. We associate it with reckless daredevils who participate in extreme sports or take other unnecessary risks. We might admire their courage but question their judgment. Courage is part of the celebrated persona of people on the edge. But are some really that fearless? No. Everyone is afraid. People are just afraid of different things. Fear keeps some people in the interior. And a different kind of fear drives some people to the edge. They go to the edge because they are afraid of leaving things as they are. They are afraid that if they don't go no one will. They are more afraid of not expanding the horizon than they are of falling off the edge.

Those leaders pay a price. Whether you are an entrepreneur, real estate developer, inventor, church planter, turnaround executive, medical researcher, politician running for office, coach, or raiser of children: converting the edge takes courage.

Converting the edge takes courage.

And converting the edge takes an incredible and sustained burst of mental, spiritual, and emotional energy. That is why some don't succeed. Not because they lack the courage. They lack the energy. If you have ever tried to plant a garden where none existed before, you understand. It takes a lot of energy to bust the sod, strip the roots, pick the rocks, cultivate the soil, plant the seeds, cultivate the soil again, and pull the weeds over and over and over. It never ends. The effort required fails some people's cost/benefit analysis. The juice isn't worth the squeeze.

Being the first to garden any spot is exhausting. It can seem impossible and be totally consuming. Leaders don't merely accept that responsibility. They own it through and through. They believe the impossible just takes longer. Christian leaders believe that with God, nothing is impossible. They pour themselves into it because they feel so deeply the duty to return to God something more than he gave them.

Leaders don't merely accept that responsibility.

Handing him back one talent clean and well-kept just isn't an option. They are poured out as a result. Because they pour out so much, others are able to pour out a little more.

The apostle Paul was on the leading edge of mission work for the early church. He suffered for the gospel. He knew what it meant to be a living sacrifice. **"But even if I am being poured out like a drink offering on the sacrifice and service coming from your faith, I am glad and rejoice with all**

of you" (Philippians 2:17). He spent himself to enable others to spend themselves. His greater sacrifice enabled others to make lesser sacrifices. Not everyone could have done that. That is why God called petulant Saul to become Paul. He was the one. He had what God needed, even if he was misusing it. But he misused it better than anyone. Once God converted him, Paul could convert many others with that same drive and determination better directed.

Sometimes leaders are viewed suspiciously. People who have everything invested in the status quo are uncomfortable with the idea that the edge could become the new middle ground. They have too much to lose. I doubt many typewriter repairmen were among the first to buy computers.

The politics of it all can be brutal. It was for a leader named Jephthah (Judges 11). He lived during a lawless time in Israel's history when "everyone did what he saw fit." Every so often, God would raise a leader to set things right. Jephthah was one of those. He was an unlikely candidate, and it wasn't easy for him. He was the illegitimate son of a philandering father and a prostitute. That immediately put him at the edge of the family. The pure-blooded brothers in Gilead drove him away so he wouldn't get any inheritance. Jephthah left and became the leader of a band of mercenaries. It wasn't until the Ammonites made war against Israel that the elders realized they were going to need this tough renegade. When they were in a desperate situation, he was good enough. That is another price some leaders pay. They are not appreciated until changing circumstances prove their worth. Jephthah did return and delivered his small-minded brothers. His vows demonstrate that he took God very seriously. He suffered the injustice of being rejected and then being needed but never rubbed his brothers' noses in it. His integrity was greater than theirs.

Harriet Tubman knew a different kind of injustice. It was the injustice of being dehumanized because of skin color. Slavery is intolerable. There is no defense for its cruelty, its underlying assumptions about the relative worth of different kinds of people, or the damage it does to the psyche of master and servant alike. Harriet had a visceral understanding of its horrors. She had to do something about it. That is what some leaders are compelled to do. Something! They take that responsibility very personally. She couldn't wait around for society to grow a conscience. She couldn't cast a paper vote for change at a polling place. And even if she could, it is unlikely that would have assuaged the moral indignation that gnawed at her. Harriet did what Thoreau later agitated for people to do. She cast her whole vote. She used her whole influence. She threw herself into it. She took matters into her own hands.

Apparently, Tubman's hands were large and

strong for a woman her size. Fieldwork made her that way. And a brush with death made her determined to risk her life to lead people to freedom. Like Moses before her, she tried to stop a fellow slave from being beaten. She was hit in the head with a heavy weight that left her with a dent in her skull and bizarre mental spells that she attributed to the Almighty. Now she was strong, motivated, and a little crazy—all necessary qualities in a leader.

Harriet voted with her whole life. She escaped to the North and then returned to the South time and again to rescue family, friends, and others. Sometimes she would literally carry fearful and reluctant slaves to freedom with those large strong hands. And she never lost a soul who came into her care. Everyone she took under her wing was liberated. She was illiterate and brilliant. She was righteous and an outlaw. In the South she was wanted dead or alive, and in the North she remained a ghost in the shadows of the Underground Railroad. She acted more than she talked. She let others worry about the legal, social, and political implications of emancipation. She devoted herself to

That was her responsibility. And she could not separate it from her trust in God.

bringing yet another black slave to freedom. That was her responsibility. And she could not separate it from her trust in God. She told her biographer,

"*I had reasoned dis out in my mind; there was one of two things I had a right to, liberty or death. If I could not have one, I would have de oder; for no man should take me alive. I should fight for my liberty as long as my strength lasted, and when de time came for me to go, de Lord would let dem take me*" (Gary Wills, *Certain Trumpets*, page 42).

I will take responsibility until God takes me. That was Tubman's resolve. And it is the mantra of Christian leaders, those in the headlines and those behind the scenes. It shatters any inclination to brush things off. It exposes the hypocrisy of griping. It looks past the facade of idle figureheads. Christian leaders take God at his Word, and they take responsibility. They don't blame the system; they become system proof. They don't lament that all is lost. They find a way to win. When the end is near, they see a new beginning is nearer. They find more to be for and less to be against. They make no excuses and shift no blame. They hold no one to higher standards than they hold themselves. They seek a good greater than their own. Their commitment is the same no matter the endeavor. *I will take responsibility until God takes me.*

I hope by now you are wondering where you could break some new ground. Is there an edge for you? Is there a controversial issue, an injustice, a lost soul, humanitarian need, dirty street, unsafe neighborhood, polluted lake, or household in disarray where by taking responsibility you could make a difference? Absolutely! Because nothing takes care of itself, and every garden needs tending. Sure, not all people are cut out to convert every edge. But there are fields of responsibility for everyone. And you can demonstrate your trust in God by owning one.

By God's design no one embodies everything that you do. And by God's plan, no one is where you are all the time. Because that is true, there are edges for you to convert. There is divine purpose in your existence. Not all edges get the same publicity. But all are worthy of someone's attention, and everyone would benefit by your decision to convert that edge. Sometimes God brings the edge to us on the feet of a child just needing a decent example to follow. The edge may approach us through promotion within an organization that needs someone to be more productive. The edge stares at us through the eyes of disturbed family members who need a calming influence in their lives. Maybe you can push your home church over the edge to become a vibrant center of grace.

And sometimes we go looking for the edge because something in us is unfulfilled. There is motivation pressing for expression. There is a song we must sing, a program we must initiate, an invention we must patent, a question we must answer, a journey we must take, a book we must write. We look for approval for our initiative on the face of Jesus.

Responding to the call of leadership is an edge in itself. We need to convert our own misgivings. Leaders have to overcome creeping self-doubt. I'm sure many highly successful people were tempted to take a nap until the impulse to do something big went away. Groundbreaking people have to confront the scariest uncertainty of all. What if it works? What if this thing takes off? What if this garden explodes? What will we do with all the fruit?

Reluctance is a common characteristic of good leaders. Remember Moses (Exodus 4)? God called him to lead his people to the Promised Land, but they would have to cross rivers and confront other challenges to get there. Moses was a humble man, and he had some serious misgivings. He tried to tell God, "I don't think I'm your guy." But Moses was the only name on God's short list of candidates, and God equipped Moses to get the job done. If you are drawn to an edge reluctantly, that's a good indication it's the right one for you.

It has been called the "Jonah complex": hearing God's call and heading the other way. It is having a sense of God's destiny for your life but thinking it's too much rigmarole. Thomas Edison is famous for saying, "Genius is one percent inspiration and ninety-nine percent perspiration." He also said, "We often miss opportunity because it's dressed in overalls and looks like work."

It will always be hard work, but we can make changes for the better in our own lives, for the welfare of our families, in the effectiveness of our churches, and to have a better world. It is the energizing possibility that greets us every morning. It is the sacred use we make of the formidable power of intention and follow-through that God has given each of us.

Finally, living itself is an edgy proposition. The causes of death come out of life. More is demanded from us to jump headfirst into a full life than succumb to the alternative. Every day we trust God's grace and providence so that we can live with confidence. Every day we take responsibility for things great and small as his faithful gardeners. Every day the edges in life threaten us and taunt us to back away. But we take the leap because we would rather be buried at the edge than left for dead somewhere else.

> Every day we take responsibility for things great and small as his faithful gardeners.

A Page for You

Where do you like to go most of the time—to the interior or to the edge?

What are the untapped opportunities in your life, family, church, or world?

How could you break some new ground to take advantage of them?

Who has inspired you with their courage?

What would it take for you to be the someone who does something when no one else will?

Prayer

Holy God, powerful God, loving God, we trust you. You have never given us a reason not to. But we confess that trust doesn't come easy for us. We are suspicious by nature, and experiences have made us cynical. We have our doubts. We let our minds run down scary paths. It's hard to call them back. Please understand we don't just have doubts about you. We have doubts about ourselves. We have doubts about other people. We have doubts about the big institutions that should be creating stability so we can feel secure. But they are among the reasons we doubt.

God of grace, give us confidence, because every promise you make you keep. Immediate uncertainties depress us, so help us see the big picture. Help us dispense with temptation and doubt the same way Jesus did: by remembering what is written in the Scriptures and by speaking your words in the face of everything that tries to take us down.

We promise we won't become arrogant, but we ask you to unleash all the power you have given us to improve things in our own lives, our families, our churches, our government, our environment, and anything we can get our minds around and our hands on. Let us see where we can act alone, and make us easy to work with when we assemble with others to solve problems.

Don't let us shy away from looking at Jesus on the cross. Revive us because all his pain, all his passion, and his last breath were for us. Help us remember that his tomb is abandoned real estate and he can overcome anything. Help us see him on his golden throne ruling for our good. Helps us be bold because he is with us.

Holy God, powerful God, loving God, we do trust you. And we are ready to accept every responsibility you give us. Amen.